Creeper, Zombie, Skeleton and Steve Jokes for Kids

by Steve Adamson

D1352984

Creeper, Zombie, Skeleton and Steve Jokes for Kids

Copyright 2014 Steve Adamson

1.

What contests do Endermen hate?

Staring contests!

2.

Why did Steve not believe the skeleton would attack him?

Because it was gutless!

3.

What do Minecraft hipsters say?

Can you dig it?

4.

What did Steve say to the skeleton trying to open his door?

You'll lever pull that!

5.

What do you get if you cross Minecraft spiders with flowers?

I don't know but don't try smelling them!

6.

What are the heaviest creatures in Minecraft?

Skele-tons!

7.

What's the difference between Steve and an archaeologist?

Archaeologists are happy to find skeletons underground!

8.

What happened when Steve accidentally spawned a wither?

He didn't know wither to laugh or cry!

9.

What did Steve sleep on at the bottom of the mine?

Bed-rock!

10.

What goes SSSsssss.....pfft?

A soggy creeper!

11.

What did the Ghast say when Steve was rude to his friend?

Nether mind him!

12.

Why should you never eat creepers?

They can cause explosive diarrhea!

13.

What did the excited rail track rider say?

"Wow I can feel my cart pounding!"

14.

What did Steve say when he faced a second wave of zombies?

It's time to take it up a Notch!

15.

How did the female Creeper excuse herself at the party?

Wait there, I've gunpowder my nose!

16.

On which day are you most likely to be killed by a zombie?

Chewsday!

17.

What do you call a small slime?

A slim!

18.

Why should you never tell pigs your Minecraft secrets?

They always squeal!

19.

What did the creeper instructor say to the Creeper recruits?

Now, watch carefully I'm only going to show you this once!

20.

What do you call a speedy Minecraft pig with a saddle?

A road hog!

21.

How does Steve get his exercise?

He runs around the block!

22.

What are the unhappiest creatures in Minecraft?

Horses – because they always have long faces!

23.

Why do cows enjoy note blocks?

They love moo-sic!

24.

Why do Minecraft horses eat with their mouths open?

They have no stable manners!

25.

How did the Nether mob feel the first time it saw Steve?

It was a-ghast!

26.

Why did the skeleton not go to the party?

He had no body to go with!

27.

What do Minecraft authors suffer from?

Writers block!

28.

What did Steve say to his girlfriend?

You stole 9.5 of my hearts!

29.

What is your rating of Minecraft?

Top-Notch!

30.

How do you know Minecraft spiders are really angry all the time?

They are always going up the wall!

31.

What did the Minecraft turkey say?

Cobble cobble!

32.

What sound do Creepers and cows make?

MoooSSSSsssss!

33.

What was the Creeper's favorite subject at school?

Hisssssstory!

34.

What did the sheep say to Steve when he took its wool?

Sheariously?

35.

Why did the Creeper cross the road?

To get to the other SSSsssside!

36.

Why did the Creeper cross the playground?

To get to the other SSSssssslide!

37.

Why did the piece of gum cross the Minecraft farm?

It was stuck to the Creeper's foot!

38.

Why did the Minecraft pig cross the road?

To prove it wasn't chicken!

39.

Why did the chicken cross the road?

What road? There are no roads in Minecraft!

40.

Why did the Enderman cross the road?

He didn't – he teleported!

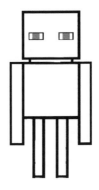

41.

What do you get if you use karate on a Minecraft pig?

A pork chop!

42.

Why couldn't the pork chop get served at his local bar?

They don't serve food!

43.

Why can't Steve get served at his local bar?

They don't serve miners!

44.

Where does an Enderman sleep?

Anywhere it wants!

45.

What did the squid say when Steve blew out his birthday candles?

Make a fish!

46.

What did Steve say to stop the skeleton killing him?

I must bow down to you!

47.

How do Minecraft pigs greet animals that moo?

Cow are you doing!

48.

Why are spiders so terrifying?

They can scare people out of their mines!

49.

What do you call a little frozen dog in the polar biome?

A pupsicle!

50.

How many Minecraft players does it take to screw in a light bulb?

None, Minecrafters use torches!

51.

What's the unluckiest kind of cat to have protecting you from Creepers?

A cat-astrophe!

52.

What is Minecraft's best-loved sport?

Boxing!

53.

What is your Minecraft pet cat's favorite color?

Purrrple!

54.

How do Creepers tell each other to be quiet?

SSShhhhhhh!

55.

What is the best horse to take into the hellish Nether?

A night-mare!

56.

What did Steve say when the Ghast killed him?

Oh that's just ghastly!

57.

How do zombies greet Steve?

Pleased to eat you!

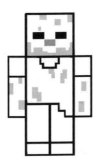

58.

Why are Ghasts always so miserable?

They find everything ghastly!

59.

What is a Creeper's favorite game at recess?

Hide and go SSSssssseek!

60..

What happened to Steve when he went through the final portal?

He reached the End!

61.

Why is cobblestone so good?

It's hand-picked!

62.

What would you get in Minecraft if you crossed a pig and a cactus?

A porky-pine

63.

What would you get if you could crossed a Creeper and a monkey?

A Ba-BOOOM!

64.

Why don't Blazes have employees?

They keep firing them!

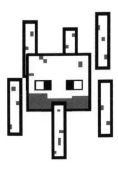

65.

What did the hoe say when it hit Steve?

Hoe do you like it?

66.

How do you know when your friends are playing too much Minecraft?

When you shout "CREEPER!" at recess everyone ducks for cover!

67.

Why are Creepers so much fun?

They are always having a blast!

68.

What mob will slow down your computer?

Renderman!

69.

Why did Steve never do well at school?

He always got mental blocks!

70.

How do you confuse a Minecrafter?

Put two shovels in a chest and tell him to take his pick!

71.

What are the dangers of mixing TNT with chickens?

They might eggs-plode!

72.

What happened in Minecraft when Jeb mixed pork with oaks?

Everyone said "Wow that's a pig tree!"

73.

What happened to the strange colored sheep?

It dyed!

74.

Why did Steve feel ill?

He had a blocked up nose!

75.

Which part of Minecraft do the Dutch like best?

The Nether-lands!

76.

What did the teacher say to the curious jungle cat?

You sure do ocelot of questions!

77.

Why do horses often die in Minecraft?

Because there are no horsepitals in Minecraft!

78.

Why are Steve's pets always being eaten in the Nether?

Ghasts love hot dogs!

79.

What do you get when you cross a zombie with a snowman?

Frostbite!

80.

What happened when Steve saw the Nether for the first time?

He was flabber-ghast-ed!

81.

What did Steve ask the Minecraft tree?

I need to axe you a question!

82.

What happens when you cross Notch's brother with a pig?

You find heroswine!

83

What did the dirt block say to Steve?

Why you always picking on me?

84.

What did the squid say to Steve?

It's a boat time you found me!

85.

What did the unhappy Ghast say?

Will I nether get out of here?

86.

How did the Minecraft witch kill you?

Her potions just brew you away!

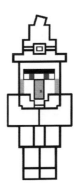

87.

What did the cow say to the other cow in the elevator?

There isn't mushroom in here!

88.

Why are there no Endermen posters on the forums?

No-one can look at them!

89.

Which glass of salty water saves the day?

Herobrine!

90.

What do only the cleverest Minecraft players solve?

Rubiks Magma Cubes!

91.

What are Minecraft spider's webs good for?

Minecraft spiders!

92.

Why should Minecraft spiders be able to swim?

They have webbed feet!

93.

What happened when Steve got killed in the Nether?

He vowed nether to go there again!

94.

What did the French skeleton say to Steve's dog?

Bone-appetite

95.

Why do hipsters hate Minecraft?

It's full of squares!

96.

Which mob serves drinks in Minecraft?

Bartenderman!

97.

What happened when a Creeper failed to sneak up on a player?

He blew his chance

98.

Why do pigs often die in Minecraft?

There are no hambulances in Minecraft!

99.

Why does Minecraft have so few bugs?

The spiders eat them all!

100.

Why is Belgium filled with lava?

Because it is next to the Nether lands!

101.

Why can't the ender dragon read any more of this book?

Because he is at The End!

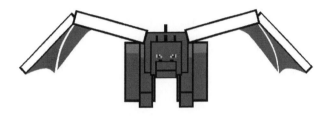

I Hope You Enjoyed the Book!

I hope you enjoyed the book. If it's given you a taste for fun you can visit our great and growing free online collection to enjoy some top-class, silly, fun and funny memes, cartoons and comics at:

http://www.pinterest.com/ipfactly/funny-minecraft/

Printed in Great Britain
by Amazon.co.uk, Ltd.,
Marston Gate.